LES PETITS PLATS
FRANÇAIS
SIMON & SCHUSTER
ILLUSTRATED

marvellous mini cakes

ILONA CHOVANCOVA

Photography by Ilona Chovancova

SIMON &
SCHUSTER

London · New York · Sydney · Toronto
A CBS COMPANY

English language edition published in Great Britain by
Simon and Schuster UK Ltd, 2010
A CBS Company

Copyright © Marabout 2010

SIMON AND SCHUSTER ILLUSTRATED BOOKS
Simon & Schuster UK
222 Gray's Inn Road
London WC1X 8HB
www.simonandschuster.co.uk

The right of Ilona Chovancova to be identified as the Author of this Work has
been asserted by her in accordance with sections 77 and 78 of the Copyright,
Designs and Patents Act, 1988.

1 2 3 4 5 6 7 8 9 10

Translation: Prudence Ivey
Copy editor English language: Nicki Lampon

Colour reproduction by Dot Gradations Ltd, UK
Printed and bound in U.A.E.

ISBN 978-0-85720-107-2

Contents

The basics

Utensils

You will need a large mixing bowl, a whisk, a wooden spoon, mini cake moulds, greaseproof paper, a skewer to check the cooking and a brush to grease the moulds with butter.

Preparing your cake moulds

Brush the moulds with butter and leave them in the freezer for 2 minutes. Dust them with flour after removing them from the freezer as it will stick to the cold butter more uniformly and will not make lumps. If there is too much flour on the moulds, the cakes won't rise properly.

To line your moulds, you can also use greaseproof paper. It is a little trickier than the first technique, but turning out your cake will be child's play. Cut a strip of paper to fit the mould lengthways and another to fit its width. Grease each mould and cover the bottom with the lengthwise strip of paper. Add the other strip so that they form a cross that covers the whole mould. This should be easy as the butter will stick the paper to the mould.

If you use silicone moulds, you won't need to do anything as they are ready to use.

Baking powder

You can add the baking powder to the cake mixture at the last minute, as the reaction that makes the mix rise won't happen while the powder is dry. This means that you can prepare the mixture without adding the baking powder, put it in the fridge and then add the baking powder just before cooking.

Filling your moulds

If you are using individual moulds, do not fill them all the way but only around two-thirds full, otherwise they may overflow.

Quantities

The quantity of cake mix is generally intended to make:

4 mini cakes measuring 64 × 110 × 45 mm (2½ x 4¼ x 1¾ inches)

6 mini cakes measuring 48 × 90 × 30 mm (2 x 3½ x 1¼ inches)

If you add a quarter of the ingredients again and 1 extra egg, you should have enough mix to make 1 large loaf cake (26 cm/10¼ inches long).

Cooking

The cooking time given with each recipe is just a guideline. It is always best to check the cakes in the last 5 minutes with a skewer (if the mini cake is cooked, the skewer should come out dry).

The cakes will cook more uniformly if you use metal moulds. The mix will rise more easily and the cakes will come out a deeper colour.

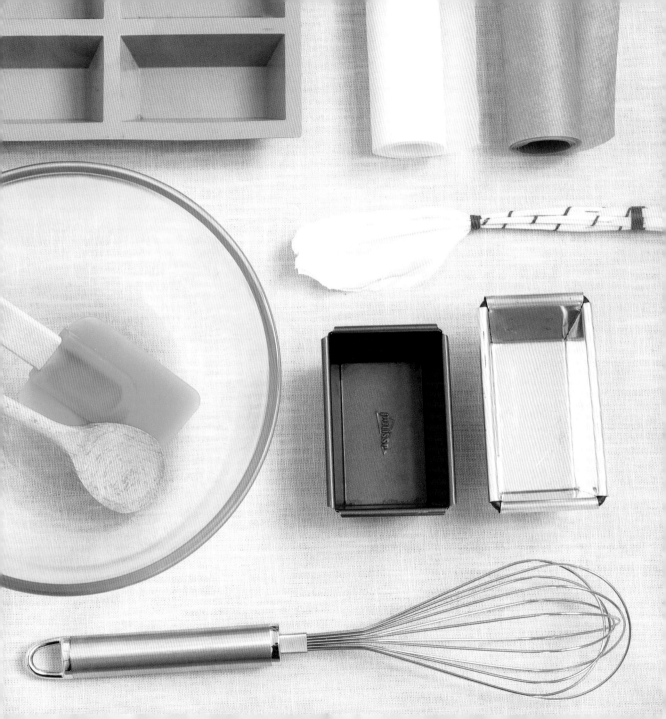

Mini cakes with carrots and bacon

Preparation time: 15 minutes
Cooking time: 30 minutes
Makes 4–6 mini cakes

Base ingredients
2 eggs
70 ml (2½ fl oz) olive oil
70 ml (2½ fl oz) milk
120 g (4¼ oz) plain flour, sifted
80 g (2¾ oz) grated Gruyère cheese
1 teaspoon baking powder
salt and pepper

Flavourings
1 carrot, grated
70 g (2½ oz) lardons (bacon pieces)
a handful of parsley, finely chopped

Preheat the oven to 180°C (fan oven 160°C), Gas Mark 4.

Grease your cake moulds and dust with flour.

In a bowl, lightly beat the eggs with the oil and milk. Add the flour, cheese, carrot, lardons and parsley. Season and stir together. Add the baking powder.

As soon as you have stirred in the baking powder, divide the mixture between the moulds and put in the oven straight away.

Cook for around 30 minutes. Towards the end of the cooking time, keep an eye on the cakes and prick with a skewer if they seem ready. If it comes out clean, the cakes are done.

Leave in the tins to cool slightly before turning out.

Oriental mini cakes with peppers and cumin

Preparation time: 15 minutes
Cooking time: 30 minutes
Makes 4–6 mini cakes

Base ingredients
2 eggs
70 ml (2½ fl oz) olive oil
70 ml (2½ fl oz) milk
120 g (4¼ oz) plain flour, sifted
80 g (2¾ oz) grated Gruyère cheese
1 teaspoon baking powder
salt and pepper

Flavourings
½ a red pepper
½ a yellow pepper
½ teaspoon ground cumin

Preheat the oven to 180°C (fan oven 160°C), Gas Mark 4.

Grease your cake moulds and dust with flour.

Wash and de-seed the peppers and cut into small pieces.

In a bowl, lightly beat the eggs with the oil and milk. Add the flour, cheese, three-quarters of the peppers (save the rest for garnish) and the ground cumin. Season and stir together. Add the baking powder.

As soon as you have stirred in the baking powder, divide the mixture between the moulds, garnish with the remaining peppers and put in the oven straight away.

Cook for around 30 minutes. Towards the end of the cooking time, keep an eye on the cakes and prick with a skewer if they seem ready. If it comes out clean, the cakes are done.

Leave in the tins to cool slightly before turning out.

Mini cakes with Parmesan and nuts

Preparation time: 10 minutes
Cooking time: 30 minutes
Makes 4–6 mini cakes

Base ingredients
2 eggs
70 ml (2½ fl oz) olive oil
70 ml (2½ fl oz) milk
140 g (5 oz) plain flour, sifted
70 g (2½ oz) grated Gruyère cheese
1 teaspoon baking powder
salt

Flavourings
50 g (1¾ oz) Parmesan cheese,
  crumbled into large chunks
70 g (2½ oz) grated Parmesan
  cheese
6 peppercorns (black or Szechuan),
  ground to a rough powder
a handful of walnuts, roughly
  chopped

Preheat the oven to 180°C (fan oven 160°C), Gas Mark 4.

Grease your cake moulds and dust with flour.

In a bowl, lightly beat the eggs with the oil and milk. Add the flour, Gruyère cheese, both lots of Parmesan cheese, the ground peppercorns and the walnuts. Season with salt and stir together. Add the baking powder.

As soon as you have stirred in the baking powder, divide the mixture between the moulds and put in the oven straight away.

Cook for around 30 minutes. Towards the end of the cooking time, keep an eye on the cakes and prick with a skewer if they seem ready. If it comes out clean, the cakes are done.

Leave in the tins to cool slightly before turning out.

Tip: You can also keep aside a quarter of the crumbled Parmesan cheese and sprinkle it on the mini cakes just before cooking.

Mini cakes with goats' cheese and grapes

Preparation time: 10 minutes
Cooking time: 30 minutes
Makes 4–6 mini cakes

Base ingredients
2 eggs
70 ml (2½ fl oz) olive oil
70 ml (2½ fl oz) milk
120 g (4¼ oz) plain flour, sifted
1 teaspoon baking powder
salt and pepper

Flavourings
a sprig of fresh rosemary
60 g (2 oz) goats' cheese, cut into
  pieces
10–15 seedless black grapes or
  100 g (3½ oz) blackcurrants

Preheat the oven to 180°C (fan oven 160°C), Gas Mark 4.

Grease your cake moulds and dust with flour.

Pull the rosemary leaves off the stalks. Set aside a few whole leaves to garnish and chop the remainder finely.

In a bowl, lightly beat the eggs with the oil and milk. Add the flour, cheese, grapes and chopped rosemary. Season and stir together. Add the baking powder.

As soon as you have stirred in the baking powder, divide the mixture between the moulds, sprinkle with the whole rosemary leaves and put in the oven straight away. Don't sink the grapes or rosemary into the mixture – they should be visible after cooking, making your cakes more attractive.

Cook for around 30 minutes. Towards the end of the cooking time, keep an eye on the cakes and prick with a skewer if they seem ready. If it comes out clean, the cakes are done.

Leave in the tins to cool slightly before turning out.

Mini cakes with Mimolette and caraway

Preparation time: 10 minutes
Cooking time: 30 minutes
Makes 4–6 mini cakes

Base ingredients
2 eggs
60 ml (2 fl oz) olive oil
70 ml (2½ fl oz) milk
120 g (4¼ oz) plain flour, sifted
1 teaspoon baking powder
salt and pepper

Flavourings
80 g (2¾ oz) grated Mimolette cheese (or Edam if you can't find Mimolette)
80 g (2¾ oz) Mimolette cheese, cut into pieces
1–2 teaspoons caraway seeds

Preheat the oven to 180°C (fan oven 160°C), Gas Mark 4.

Grease your cake moulds and dust with flour.

In a bowl, lightly beat the eggs with the oil and milk. Add the flour, both lots of Mimolette cheese and the caraway seeds. Season and stir together. Add the baking powder.

As soon as you have stirred in the baking powder, divide the mixture between the moulds and put in the oven straight away.

Cook for around 30 minutes. Towards the end of the cooking time, keep an eye on the cakes and prick with a skewer if they seem ready. If it comes out clean, the cakes are done.

Leave in the tins to cool slightly before turning out.

Note: Caraway seeds are a spice, a little like cumin but with a slightly less strong flavour. In India, caraway is used in curries, lentils and rice. In Eastern Europe and Germany it is used to season meat products, sauerkraut and fish. You can find caraway seeds in the spice aisle of the supermarket.

Mini cakes with bacon and sage

Preparation time: 10 minutes
Cooking time: 30 minutes
Makes 4–6 mini cakes

Base ingredients
2 eggs
70 ml (2½ fl oz) olive oil
70 ml (2½ fl oz) milk
120 g (4¼ oz) plain flour, sifted
80 g (2¾ oz) grated Gruyère cheese
1 teaspoon baking powder
salt and pepper

Flavourings
80 g (2¾ oz) lardons (bacon pieces)
3 fresh sage leaves, finely chopped

Preheat the oven to 180°C (fan oven 160°C), Gas Mark 4.

Grease your cake moulds and dust with flour.

In a bowl, lightly beat the eggs with the oil and milk. Add the flour, cheese, lardons and sage. Season and stir. Add the baking powder.

As soon as you have stirred in the baking powder, divide the mixture between the moulds and put in the oven straight away.

Cook for around 30 minutes. Towards the end of the cooking time, keep an eye on the cakes and prick with a skewer if they seem ready. If it comes out clean, the cakes are done.

Leave in the tins to cool slightly before turning out.

Mini cakes with cured meats and nuts

Preparation time: 10 minutes
Cooking time: 30 minutes
Makes 4–6 mini cakes

Base ingredients
3 eggs
100 ml (3½ fl oz) olive oil
100 ml (3½ fl oz) milk
180 g (6¼ oz) plain flour, sifted
100 g (3½ oz) grated Gruyère
  cheese
1 teaspoon baking powder
salt and pepper

Flavourings
70 g (2½ oz) salami, cut into pieces
70 g (2½ oz) chorizo, cut into pieces
a handful of hazelnuts, roughly
  chopped
20 pistachio nuts

Preheat the oven to 180°C (fan oven 160°C), Gas Mark 4.

Grease your cake moulds and dust with flour.

In a bowl, lightly beat the eggs with the oil and milk. Add the flour, cheese and three-quarters of the flavouring ingredients. Season and stir together until you have a smooth paste. Add the baking powder.

As soon as you have stirred in the baking powder, divide the mixture between the moulds. Garnish with the remaining flavouring ingredients and put in the oven straight away.

Cook for around 30 minutes. Towards the end of the cooking time, keep an eye on the cakes and prick with a skewer if they seem ready. If it comes out clean, the cakes are done.

Leave in the tins to cool slightly before turning out.

Tip: If you have a pestle and mortar you can use it to roughly break up the hazelnuts. If not, you could put them in a freezer bag and hit with a rolling pin. Either of these ways will be much easier and faster than cutting them with a knife.

Leek and bacon mini cakes

Preparation time: 10 minutes
Cooking time: 30 minutes
Makes 4–6 mini cakes

Base ingredients
2 eggs
70 ml (2½ fl oz) olive oil
70 ml (2½ fl oz) milk
80 g (2¾ oz) buckwheat flour
40 g (1½ oz) plain flour, sifted
80 g (2¾ oz) grated Gruyère cheese
1 teaspoon baking powder
salt and pepper

Flavourings
80 g (2¾ oz) smoked lardons
  (bacon pieces)
½ leek, finely chopped

Preheat the oven to 180°C (fan oven 160°C), Gas Mark 4.

Grease your cake moulds and dust with flour.

In a bowl, lightly beat the eggs with the oil and milk. Add the two flours, cheese, lardons and leek. Season and stir together. Add the baking powder.

As soon as you have stirred in the baking powder, divide the mixture between the moulds and put in the oven straight away.

Cook for around 30 minutes. Towards the end of the cooking time, keep an eye on the cakes and prick with a skewer if they seem ready. If it comes out clean, the cakes are done.

Leave in the tins to cool slightly before turning out.

Tip: These go particularly well with a cool glass of cider.

Curried chicken mini cakes

Preparation time: 15 minutes
Cooking time: 30 minutes
Makes 4–6 mini cakes

Base ingredients
2 eggs
70 ml (2½ fl oz) olive oil
70 ml (2½ fl oz) milk
120 g (4¼ oz) plain flour, sifted
70 g (2½ oz) grated Gruyère cheese
1 teaspoon baking powder
salt and pepper

Flavourings
1 teaspoon curry powder
100 g (3½ oz) cooked chicken, cut
   into pieces

Preheat the oven to 180°C (fan oven 160°C), Gas Mark 4.

Grease your cake moulds and dust with flour.

In a bowl, lightly beat the eggs with the oil and milk. Add the flour, curry powder, cheese and chicken. Season and stir. Add the baking powder.

As soon as you have stirred in the baking powder, divide the mixture between the moulds and put in the oven straight away.

Cook for around 30 minutes. Towards the end of the cooking time, keep an eye on the cakes and prick with a skewer if they seem ready. If it comes out clean, the cakes are done.

Leave in the tins to cool slightly before turning out.

Tip: You can also add a handful of finely chopped parsley to this recipe.

Mini cakes with mustard and tarragon

Preparation time: 10 minutes
Cooking time: 30 minutes
Makes 4–6 mini cakes

Base ingredients
2 eggs
80 ml (2¾ fl oz) olive oil
80 ml (2¾ fl oz) milk
140 g (5 oz) plain flour, sifted
80 g (2¾ oz) grated Gruyère cheese
1 teaspoon baking powder
salt and pepper

Flavourings
1 dessertspoon wholegrain mustard
a small bunch of fresh tarragon,
    finely chopped

Preheat the oven to 180°C (fan oven 160°C), Gas Mark 4.

Grease your cake moulds and dust with flour.

In a bowl, lightly beat the eggs with the oil, milk and mustard. Add the flour, cheese and tarragon. Season and stir. Add the baking powder.

As soon as you have stirred in the baking powder, divide the mixture between the moulds and put in the oven straight away.

Cook for around 30 minutes. Towards the end of the cooking time, keep an eye on the cakes and prick with a skewer if they seem ready. If it comes out clean, the cakes are done.

Leave in the tins to cool slightly before turning out.

Tip: You could use capers instead of the tarragon.

Mini cakes with black olives and sun-dried tomatoes

Preparation time: 15 minutes
Cooking time: 30 minutes
Makes 4–6 mini cakes

Base ingredients
2 eggs
70 ml (2½ fl oz) olive oil
70 ml (2½ fl oz) milk
120 g (4¼ oz) plain flour, sifted
70 g (2½ oz) grated Gruyère cheese
1 teaspoon baking powder
salt and pepper

Flavourings
100 g (3½ oz) sun-dried tomatoes,
   roughly chopped
100 g (3½ oz) pitted black olives

Preheat the oven to 180°C (fan oven 160°C), Gas Mark 4.

Grease your cake moulds and dust with flour.

In a bowl, lightly beat the eggs with the oil and milk. Add the flour, cheese, sun-dried tomatoes and olives (setting aside a few to garnish the cakes). Season and stir together. Add the baking powder.

As soon as you have stirred in the baking powder, divide the mixture between the moulds. Slice the remaining olives and arrange on the surface of the cakes. Put in the oven straight away.

Cook for around 30 minutes. Towards the end of the cooking time, keep an eye on the cakes and prick with a skewer if they seem ready. If it comes out clean, the cakes are done.

Leave in the tins to cool slightly before turning out.

Pumpkin and Parmesan mini cakes

Preparation time: 15 minutes
Cooking time: 30 minutes
Makes 4–6 mini cakes

Base ingredients
2 eggs
70 ml (2½ fl oz) olive oil
70 ml (2½ fl oz) milk
120 g (4¼ oz) plain flour, sifted
70 g (2½ oz) grated Gruyère cheese
1 teaspoon baking powder
salt and pepper

Flavourings
100 g (3½ oz) pumpkin
100 g (3½ oz) grated Parmesan
  cheese
3 fresh sage leaves, finely chopped

Preheat the oven to 180°C (fan oven 160°C), Gas Mark 4.

Grease your cake moulds and dust with flour.

Roughly grate the pumpkin flesh. Squeeze the grated flesh in the palm of your hand to remove the excess liquid.

In a bowl, lightly beat the eggs with the oil, milk, pumpkin and Parmesan cheese. Add the flour, Gruyère cheese and sage. Season and stir together. Add the baking powder.

As soon as you have stirred in the baking powder, divide the mixture between the moulds and put in the oven straight away.

Cook for around 30 minutes. Towards the end of the cooking time, keep an eye on the cakes and prick with a skewer if they seem ready. If it comes out clean, the cakes are done.

Leave in the tins to cool slightly before turning out.

Tip: If you use a small, squash-like pumpkin, you should not need to peel it as the skin should be fairly soft. It should be enough just to quarter, de-seed and then grate it right away. If you use a larger pumpkin you will need to peel it first.

Courgette and Parmesan mini cakes

Preparation time: 15 minutes
Cooking time: 30 minutes
Makes 4–6 mini cakes

Base ingredients
2 eggs
70 ml (2½ fl oz) olive oil
70 ml (2½ fl oz) milk
120 g (4¼ oz) plain flour, sifted
70 g (2½ oz) grated Gruyère cheese
70 g (2½ oz) grated Parmesan
  cheese
1 teaspoon baking powder
salt and pepper

Flavourings
a handful of fresh basil, finely
  chopped
a handful of fresh mint, finely
  chopped
1 courgette, finely grated

Preheat the oven to 180°C (fan oven 160°C), Gas Mark 4.

Grease your cake moulds and dust with flour.

In a bowl, lightly beat the eggs with the oil and milk. Add the flour, both cheeses, basil and mint. Squeeze the grated courgette in the palm of your hand to remove the excess water and add to the mixture. Season and stir together. Add the baking powder.

As soon as you have stirred in the baking powder, divide the mixture between the moulds and put in the oven straight away.

Cook for around 30 minutes. Towards the end of the cooking time, keep an eye on the cakes and prick with a skewer if they seem ready. If it comes out clean, the cakes are done.

Leave in the tins to cool slightly before turning out.

Tip: You can cut a piece of the courgette into fine slices and use to garnish the cakes.

Roquefort, pear and walnut mini cakes

Preparation time: 15 minutes
Cooking time: 30 minutes
Makes 4–6 mini cakes

Base ingredients
2 eggs
70 ml (2½ fl oz) olive oil
70 ml (2½ fl oz) milk
120 g (4¼ oz) plain flour, sifted
70 g (2½ oz) grated Gruyère cheese
1 teaspoon baking powder
salt and pepper

Flavourings
100 g (3½ oz) Roquefort cheese,
  crumbled
1 small pear, peeled, cored and cut
  into small pieces
2 handfuls of walnuts, roughly
  chopped

Preheat the oven to 180°C (fan oven 160°C), Gas Mark 4.

Grease your cake moulds and dust with flour.

In a bowl, lightly beat the eggs with the oil and milk. Add the flour, both cheeses, pear and walnuts. Season and stir. Add the baking powder.

As soon as you have stirred in the baking powder, divide the mixture between the moulds and put in the oven straight away.

Cook for around 30 minutes. Towards the end of the cooking time, keep an eye on the cakes and prick with a skewer if they seem ready. If it comes out clean, the cakes are done.

Leave in the tins to cool slightly before turning out.

Maize flour and poppy seed mini cakes

Preparation time: 15 minutes
Cooking time: 30 minutes
Makes 4–6 mini cakes

Base ingredients
2 eggs
40 ml (1½ fl oz) olive oil
100 ml (3½ fl oz) buttermilk
150 g (5¼ oz) maize flour
1 dessertspoon poppy seeds
1 teaspoon baking powder
salt and pepper

Flavourings
(see Tip)

Preheat the oven to 180°C (fan oven 160°C), Gas Mark 4.

Grease your cake moulds and dust with flour.

In a bowl, lightly beat the eggs with the oil and buttermilk. Add the flour and poppy seeds. Season and stir together. Add the baking powder.

As soon as you have stirred in the baking powder, divide the mixture between the moulds and put in the oven straight away.

Cook for around 30 minutes. Towards the end of the cooking time, keep an eye on the cakes and prick with a skewer if they seem ready. If it comes out clean, the cakes are done.

Leave in the tins to cool slightly before turning out.

Tip: Here are some additional ideas for flavouring these cakes:

Ricotta + pesto: Mix 200 g (7 oz) ricotta with 5 teaspoons of pesto.

Tuna + shallots + lemon: Mix a small tin of tuna with some finely chopped shallots. Add 3 dessertspoons of mayonnaise and season with lemon juice.

Fromage frais + chilli: Mix 150 g (5¼ oz) fromage frais with 2 teaspoons of paprika or chilli powder. Add a handful of finely chopped chives.

Cream cheese + radish + basil: Chop a bunch of radishes and mix with 150 g (5¼ oz) cream cheese. Add some roughly chopped basil.

Egg mayonnaise + fresh herbs: Finely chop 4 hard-boiled eggs. Add 50 g (1¾ oz) mayonnaise, 100 g (3½ oz) cream cheese, some chopped parsley and 1 teaspoon of mustard. Mix.

Emmental + garlic: Finely grate 150 g (5¼ oz) Emmental cheese, purée 3–4 garlic cloves and mix with 100 g (3½ oz) mayonnaise.

Mini cakes with dried figs and rosemary

Preparation time: 15 minutes
Cooking time: 30 minutes
Makes 4–6 mini cakes

Base ingredients
1 egg
40 ml (1½ fl oz) olive oil
100 ml (3½ fl oz) buttermilk
180 g (6¼ oz) spelt flour
1 teaspoon baking powder
salt

Flavourings
a large handful of dried figs, cut into
    small pieces
a few sprigs of rosemary, leaves
    finely chopped

Preheat the oven to 180°C (fan oven 160°C), Gas Mark 4.

Grease your cake moulds and dust with flour.

In a bowl, lightly beat the egg with the oil and buttermilk. Add the flour, figs and chopped rosemary. Season and stir. Add the baking powder.

As soon as you have stirred in the baking powder, divide the mixture between the moulds and put in the oven straight away.

Cook for around 30 minutes. Towards the end of the cooking time, keep an eye on the cakes and prick with a skewer if they seem ready. If it comes out clean, the cakes are done.

Leave in the tins to cool slightly before turning out.

Tip: You can also garnish the cakes with a few rosemary leaves.

Sugar-free mini cakes with chestnut flour and sesame seeds

Preparation time: 10 minutes
Cooking time: 30 minutes
Makes 4–6 mini cakes

Base ingredients
1 egg
120 ml (4¼ fl oz) buttermilk
40 ml (1½ fl oz) olive oil
30 g (1 oz) plain flour, sifted
130 g (4½ oz) chestnut flour
1 teaspoon baking powder
salt

Flavouring
1 dessertspoon sesame seeds,
  lightly toasted

Preheat the oven to 180°C (fan oven 160°C), Gas Mark 4.

Grease your cake moulds and dust with flour.

In a bowl, lightly beat the egg with the buttermilk and oil. Add both flours and the toasted sesame seeds. Season with salt and stir together. Add the baking powder.

As soon as you have stirred in the baking powder, divide the mixture between the moulds and put in the oven straight away.

Cook for around 30 minutes. Towards the end of the cooking time, keep an eye on the cakes and prick with a skewer if they seem ready. If it comes out clean, the cakes are done.

Leave in the tins to cool slightly before turning out.

Note: This type of cake has a very neutral taste and makes an ideal bread replacement for breakfast. Spread with butter and jam or add lemon curd or Nutella.

Sugar-free mini cakes with dried apricots and hazelnuts

Preparation time: 10 minutes
Cooking time: 30 minutes
Makes 4–6 mini cakes

Base ingredients
1 egg
100 ml (3½ fl oz) buttermilk
40 ml (1½ fl oz) vegetable oil
100 g (3½ oz) plain flour, sifted
50 g (1¾ oz) porridge oats
1 teaspoon baking powder
salt and pepper

Flavourings
a handful of dried apricots, cut into small pieces
a handful of hazelnuts, roughly chopped

Preheat the oven to 180°C (fan oven 160°C), Gas Mark 4.

Grease your cake moulds and dust with flour.

In a bowl, lightly beat the egg with the buttermilk and oil. Add the flour, oats, apricots and hazelnuts. Season and stir. Add the baking powder.

As soon as you have stirred in the baking powder, divide the mixture between the moulds and put in the oven straight away.

Cook for around 30 minutes. Towards the end of the cooking time, keep an eye on the cakes and prick with a skewer if they seem ready. If it comes out clean, the cakes are done.

Leave in the tins to cool slightly before turning out.

Note: These mini cakes taste quite bready. They are ideal for breakfast or as a teatime snack with a little jam or butter.

Mini pound cakes with strawberry jam

Preparation time: 15 minutes
Cooking time: 30 minutes
Makes 4–6 mini cakes

Base ingredients
120 g (4¼ oz) salted butter
120 g (4¼ oz) caster sugar
2 eggs, separated
120 g (4¼ oz) plain flour, sifted
2 scant teaspoons baking powder
a pinch of salt

Filling
strawberry jam

Preheat the oven to 180°C (fan oven 160°C), Gas Mark 4.

Grease your cake moulds and dust with flour.

In a bowl, beat the butter and sugar together until the mixture turns pale and becomes smooth. Add the egg yolks, flour and salt and mix in.

In another bowl, whisk the egg whites. Add them gradually to the mixture. Add the baking powder.

As soon as you have stirred in the baking powder, put 1–2 dessertspoons of cake mixture in each mould. Add a teaspoon or two of jam to the centre of each cake. Cover with the remaining cake mixture, ensuring that the jam is fully covered by the cake mix. This will make the cakes easier to turn out. Put in the oven straight away.

Cook for around 30 minutes. Towards the end of the cooking time, keep an eye on the cakes and prick with a skewer if they seem ready. If it comes out clean, the cakes are done.

Leave in the tins to cool slightly before turning out.

Marmalade mini cakes

Preparation time: 20 minutes
Cooking time: 25 minutes
Makes 4–6 mini cakes

Base ingredients
2 eggs
70 g (2½ oz) brown sugar
120 g (4¼ oz) plain flour, sifted
100 g (3½ oz) butter, melted
2 scant teaspoons baking powder
a pinch of salt

Flavourings
a handful of walnuts, roughly
   chopped
3 dessertspoons thick-cut
   marmalade

Preheat the oven to 180°C (fan oven 160°C), Gas Mark 4.

Grease your cake moulds and dust with flour.

In a bowl, beat the eggs with the sugar until they become aerated and foamy. Little by little, add the flour, salt and melted butter. Add the walnuts. Stir in the marmalade but do not incorporate entirely into the mixture. Add the baking powder.

As soon as you have stirred in the baking powder, divide the mixture between the moulds and put in the oven straight away.

Cook for around 25 minutes. Towards the end of the cooking time, keep an eye on the cakes and prick with a skewer if they seem ready. If it comes out clean, the cakes are done.

Leave in the tins to cool slightly before turning out.

Mini chocolate fondants with pink peppercorn pieces

Preparation time: 15 minutes
Cooking time: 15 minutes
Makes 4–6 mini cakes

Base ingredients
250 g (9 oz) dark chocolate, broken
   into pieces
100 g (3½ oz) butter, cut into cubes
3 eggs, separated
50 g (1¾ oz) icing sugar
1 dessertspoon plain flour, sifted
a pinch of salt

Pink peppercorn caramel
100 g (3½ oz) caster sugar
2 dessertspoons water
2 drops of lemon juice
2 teaspoons pink peppercorns,
   roughly ground

Preheat the oven to 180°C (fan oven 160°C), Gas Mark 4.

Grease your cake moulds and dust with flour.

Put the chocolate and cubed butter in a large bowl. Melt in the microwave or over a pan of simmering water.

Once melted, mix the chocolate and butter together then add the egg yolks one by one. Add the icing sugar and flour.

In another bowl, whisk the egg whites with a pinch of salt then add little by little to the chocolate mixture. Mix until smooth. Divide the mixture between the moulds.

Cook for around 30 minutes. Towards the end of the cooking time, keep an eye on the cakes and prick with a skewer if they seem ready. If it comes out clean, the cakes are done.

Leave in the tins to cool slightly before turning out.

While the cakes are cooking, prepare the pink peppercorn caramel. Put the sugar in a heavy-based saucepan, add the water and shake the pan to mix it in. Cook over a low heat, shaking slightly from time to time to spread the heat. Do not mix with a spoon as the sugar will melt gradually on its own. Stop cooking once the carmel is medium gold. To keep it liquid for longer, add a couple of drops of lemon juice. Add the pink peppercorns and mix. Pour the caramel on to a sheet of greaseproof paper, spread into a fine layer and leave to harden.

Once it has set, break the caramel into small pieces and then grind to a rough powder with a pestle and mortar.

Just before serving, sprinkle the caramel over the fondants.

Tip: You can also serve these as a dessert with custard or vanilla ice cream.

Mini cakes with pine nuts and honey

Preparation time: 15 minutes
Cooking time: 25 minutes
Makes 4–6 mini cakes

Base ingredients
1 egg
50 g (1¾ oz) brown sugar
50 ml (1¾ fl oz) vegetable oil
60 ml (2 fl oz) buttermilk
150 g (5¼ oz) plain flour, sifted
2 scant teaspoons baking powder
a pinch of salt

Flavourings
2 heaped dessertspoons honey
50 g (1¾ oz) pine nuts

Preheat the oven to 180°C (fan oven 160°C), Gas Mark 4.

Grease your cake moulds and dust with flour.

In a bowl, beat the egg with the sugar, oil, honey and buttermilk. Add the flour, salt and pine nuts little by little. Stir the mixture without making it completely smooth. Add the baking powder and mix in.

As soon as you have stirred in the baking powder, divide the mixture between the moulds and put in the oven straight away.

Cook for around 25 minutes. Towards the end of the cooking time, keep an eye on the cakes and prick with a skewer if they seem ready. If it comes out clean, the cakes are done.

Leave in the tins to cool slightly before turning out.

Tips: You could replace the pine nuts with pistachios.

You can make your cakes look pretty by reserving some of the pine nuts and sprinkling them over the top just before cooking.

Mini cakes with candied fruit

Preparation time: 20 minutes
Cooking time: 25 minutes
Makes 4–6 mini cakes

Base ingredients

100 g (3½ oz) butter, softened
70 g (2½ oz) brown sugar
1 egg
100 g (3½ oz) plain flour, sifted
2 scant teaspoons baking powder
a pinch of salt

Flavourings

50 g (1¾ oz) mixed candied fruit
  (orange, angelica, mandarin,
  lemon)
a handful of chopped walnuts
1 dessertspoon dark rum or cognac
  (optional)
3 black peppercorns, ground
50 g (1¾ oz) glacé cherries

Preheat the oven to 180°C (fan oven 160°C), Gas Mark 4.

Grease your cake moulds and dust with flour.

In a bowl, mix together the butter and sugar. Add the egg, flour, candied fruit (saving some for decoration), chopped nuts, salt, rum or cognac (if using) and ground peppercorns. Mix together. Add the baking powder.

As soon as you have stirred in the baking powder, divide the mixture between the moulds. Decorate them with candied fruit cut into strips and the glacé cherries and put in the oven straight away.

Cook for around 25 minutes. Towards the end of the cooking time, keep an eye on the cakes and prick with a skewer if they seem ready. If it comes out clean, the cakes are done.

Leave in the tins to cool slightly before turning out.

Chocolate and sesame mini cakes with candied orange peel

Preparation time: 15 minutes
Cooking time: 30 minutes
Makes 4–6 mini cakes

Base ingredients
100 g (3½ oz) butter
2 eggs
100 g (3½ oz) caster sugar
30 ml (1 fl oz) milk
120 g (4¼ oz) plain flour, sifted
2 scant teaspoons baking powder
a pinch of salt

Flavourings
70 g (2½ oz) dark chocolate, broken
   into small pieces
1 dessertspoon cocoa powder
1 dessertspoon sesame seeds
50 g (1¾ oz) candied orange peel,
   roughly chopped

Preheat the oven to 180°C (fan oven 160°C), Gas Mark 4.

Grease your cake moulds and dust with flour.

Melt the butter with the chocolate in the microwave or in a bowl over a pan of simmering water.

In a bowl, lightly beat the eggs with the sugar. When the mixture doubles in size and gets a mousse-like consistency, add the milk, cocoa powder, butter and chocolate mixture, flour and salt and stir. Add the sesame seeds and candied orange peel and mix again. Add the baking powder.

As soon as you have stirred in the baking powder, divide the mixture between the moulds and put in the oven straight away.

Cook for around 30 minutes. Towards the end of the cooking time, keep an eye on the cakes and prick with a skewer if they seem ready. If it comes out clean, the cakes are done.

Leave in the tins to cool slightly before turning out.

Tip: You can make your cakes look pretty by reserving some of the sesame seeds and candied orange peel and sprinkling them over the top just before cooking.

Sweet mini cakes with raspberries

Preparation time: 15 minutes
Cooking time: 25 minutes
Makes 4–6 mini cakes

Base ingredients

1 egg
100 g (3½ oz) caster sugar
100 ml (3½ fl oz) whipping cream
170 g (6 oz) plain flour, sifted
2 scant teaspoons baking powder
icing sugar for dusting

Flavouring

150 g (5¼ oz) raspberries

Preheat the oven to 180°C (fan oven 160°C), Gas Mark 4.

Grease your cake moulds and dust with flour.

In a large bowl, beat the egg with the sugar. Add the whipping cream and the flour bit by bit. Stir until smooth. Add the baking powder.

Put 1 or 2 spoonfuls of cake mix into each mould. Share half the raspberries between the moulds. Cover with the rest of the mix and decorate with the remaining raspberries.

Put in the oven right away and cook for around 25 minutes. Towards the end of the cooking time, keep an eye on the cakes and prick with a skewer if they seem ready. If it comes out clean, the cakes are done.

Leave in the tins to cool slightly before turning out. Sift over icing sugar before serving.

Tip: These cakes are also delicious using redcurrants or blueberries. If using either of these, remove from the stalks then roll the berries in flour (this will stop them sinking to the bottom of the moulds). If you use frozen berries, defrost them but make sure they stay fairly firm.

Mini cakes with yogurt filled with lemon curd

Preparation time: 20 minutes
Cooking time: 25 minutes
Makes 4–6 mini cakes

Base ingredients
125 g (4½ oz) natural yogurt
125 g (4½ oz) vegetable oil
2 eggs
250 g (9 oz) caster sugar
250 g (9 oz) plain flour, sifted
2 scant teaspoons baking powder
a pinch of salt

Lemon curd
juice of 2 lemons
200 g (7 oz) caster sugar
100 g (3½ oz) butter, cut into
  small cubes
3 eggs

Prepare the lemon curd: in a small bowl, mix together all the ingredients. Cook over a pan of simmering water for around 15 minutes. For the final 5 minutes of cooking, stir constantly to ensure the eggs do not congeal. Pour into a jar and leave to cool.

Preheat the oven to 180°C (fan oven 160°C), Gas Mark 4.

Grease your cake moulds and dust with flour.

Pour the yogurt into a large mixing bowl.

Mix in the oil, eggs, sugar and a pinch of salt. Gradually add the flour and mix until you have a smooth paste. Add the baking powder.

Add 2 good spoonfuls of cake mix to each mould. Put 1 or 2 teaspoons of lemon curd in the centre of each mould. Cover well with the remaining cake mix to ensure easy turning out. Put in the oven immediately.

Cook for around 20–25 minutes. Towards the end of the cooking time, keep an eye on the cakes and prick with a skewer if they seem ready. If it comes out clean, the cakes are done.

Leave in the tins to cool slightly before turning out.

Tip: You can use any citrus fruit for this recipe or any fruit that is quite acidic (250 g/9 oz of redcurrants or raspberries would work). If you use a soft fruit, cook over a medium heat for 5 minutes to get a purée. Pass through a fine sieve and use the juice in place of the lemon juice. If the fruit is less acidic (e.g. grapefruit, oranges, raspberries) add a few drops of lemon juice.

Poppy seed mini cakes with lemon icing

Preparation time: 25 minutes
Cooking time: 25 minutes
Makes 4–6 mini cakes

Base ingredients
2 eggs
120 g (4¼ oz) caster sugar
120 g (4¼ oz) plain flour, sifted
100 g (3½ oz) butter, melted
1 dessertspoon poppy seeds
zest and juice of 1 lemon
2 scant teaspoons baking powder
a pinch of salt

Icing ingredients
150 g (5¼ oz) icing sugar
2 dessertspoons hot water
2–3 dessertspoons lemon juice

Prepare the icing: mix the icing sugar, water and lemon juice until the icing is smooth and glossy. This will take around 10–15 minutes. The longer you work the mixture, the whiter and glossier your icing will be.

Preheat the oven to 180°C (fan oven 160°C), Gas Mark 4.

Grease your cake moulds and dust with flour.

In a bowl, beat the eggs with the sugar. When the mixture doubles in size and gets a mousse-like consistency, add the flour, melted butter, poppy seeds, salt and lemon zest and juice. Mix without allowing the paste to become fully smooth. Add the baking powder.

As soon as you have stirred in the baking powder, divide the mixture between the moulds and put in the oven straight away.

Cook for around 30 minutes. Towards the end of the cooking time, keep an eye on the cakes and prick with a skewer if they seem ready. If it comes out clean, the cakes are done.

Leave in the tins to cool slightly before turning out.

Put the cakes on a cooling rack and pour the icing over them while they are still warm. Leave to set.

Hazelnut mini cakes

Preparation time: 15 minutes
Cooking time: 30 minutes
Makes 4–6 mini cakes

Base ingredients
4 egg whites
130 g (4½ oz) icing sugar
50 g (1¾ oz) plain flour, sifted
80 g (2¾ oz) butter, melted

Flavourings
60 g (1 oz) ground hazelnuts
a small handful of hazelnuts,
  roughly chopped

Preheat the oven to 180°C (fan oven 160°C), Gas Mark 4.

Grease your cake moulds and dust with flour.

In a bowl, whisk the eggs into stiff peaks, adding the icing sugar little by little. Gently fold in the ground hazelnuts and flour then the melted butter. Pour into the moulds then sprinkle with the chopped hazelnuts.

Cook for around 25–30 minutes. Towards the end of the cooking time, keep an eye on the cakes and prick with a skewer if they seem ready. If it comes out clean, the cakes are done.

Leave in the tins to cool slightly before turning out.

Tip: You could use ground almonds instead of hazelnuts if you prefer.

Chocolate mini cakes with hazelnut filling

Preparation time: 20 minutes
Cooking time: 20 minutes
Makes 4–6 mini cakes

Base ingredients
100 g (3½ oz) butter
80 g (2¾ oz) dark chocolate, broken
   into pieces
2 eggs
100 g (3½ oz) caster sugar
120 g (4¼ oz) plain flour, sifted
1 teaspoon cocoa powder
30 ml (1 fl oz) milk
2 scant teaspoons baking powder

Filling
125 g (4½ oz) hazelnuts
125 g (4½ oz) caster sugar

Prepare the hazelnut filling: put the hazelnuts and sugar in a heavy-based saucepan. Heat over a medium heat to melt the sugar while stirring constantly. Continue to heat until the sugar turns into caramel. Once the caramel has enveloped the hazelnuts, pour on to a baking tray covered with greaseproof paper. Leave to cool. Once hardened, break into small pieces and, using an electric mixer, reduce to a smooth paste. The longer you mix it, the more liquid and oily the paste will become.

Preheat the oven to 180°C (fan oven 160°C), Gas Mark 4.

Grease your cake moulds and dust with flour.

Melt the butter with the chocolate in the microwave or in a bowl over a pan of simmering water.

In a bowl, lightly beat the eggs with the sugar. When the mixture doubles in size and gets a mousse-like consistency, add the flour little by little with the butter and chocolate mixture. Add the cocoa powder and milk and stir. Add the baking powder.

As soon as you have stirred in the baking powder, add 1 or 2 dessertspoons of the mixture to each mould. Add 1 or 2 teaspoons of hazelnut paste to the centre of each. Cover with the rest of the cake mix, making sure the hazelnut paste is well covered to ease the turning out. Put in the oven immediately.

Cook for around 20 minutes. Towards the end of the cooking time, keep an eye on the cakes and prick with a skewer if they seem ready. If it comes out clean, the cakes are done.

Leave in the tins to cool slightly before turning out.

Tip: You could replace the hazelnut paste with Nutella.

Pear and chocolate chip mini cakes

Preparation time: 15 minutes
Cooking time: 30 minutes
Makes 4–6 mini cakes

Base ingredients
1 egg
90 g (3 oz) brown sugar
80 ml (2¾ fl oz) buttermilk
50 ml (1¾ fl oz) vegetable oil
150 g (5¼ oz) plain flour, sifted
2 scant teaspoons baking powder
a pinch of salt

Flavourings
1 pear, peeled, cored and cut into
   small pieces
50 g (1¾ oz) chocolate chips

Preheat the oven to 180°C (fan oven 160°C), Gas Mark 4.

Grease your cake moulds and dust with flour.

In a bowl, lightly beat the egg with the sugar, buttermilk and oil. Gradually add the flour, salt, pieces of pear and chocolate chips. Mix without letting the paste get completely smooth. Add the baking powder.

As soon as you have stirred in the baking powder, divide the mixture between the moulds and put in the oven straight away.

Cook for around 30 minutes. Towards the end of the cooking time, keep an eye on the cakes and prick with a skewer if they seem ready. If it comes out clean, the cakes are done.

Leave in the tins to cool slightly before turning out.

Oaty mini cakes with pineapple

Preparation time: 15 minutes
Cooking time: 30 minutes
Makes 4–6 mini cakes

Base ingredients
1 egg
90 g (3 oz) brown sugar
80 ml (2¾ fl oz) buttermilk
50 ml (1¾ fl oz) olive oil
100 g (3½ oz) plain flour, sifted
50 g (1¾ oz) porridge oats
2 scant teaspoons baking powder
a pinch of salt

Flavourings
1 small tin of pineapple in syrup,
  drained and chopped into small
  pieces
a pinch of cinnamon

Preheat the oven to 180°C (fan oven 160°C), Gas Mark 4.

Grease your cake moulds and dust with flour.

In a bowl, lightly beat the egg with the sugar, buttermilk and oil. Gradually add the flour, oats, salt, pineapple and cinnamon. Keep a few pieces of pineapple aside to decorate the cakes. Stir without allowing the mixture to become completely smooth. Add the baking powder.

As soon as you have stirred in the baking powder, divide the mixture between the moulds. Decorate with the remaining pineapple and put in the oven straight away.

Cook for around 30 minutes. Towards the end of the cooking time, keep an eye on the cakes and prick with a skewer if they seem ready. If it comes out clean, the cakes are done.

Leave in the tins to cool slightly before turning out.

Tip: You could also use fresh or frozen pineapple (if frozen, defrost but do not allow to become too soft). Cut in small pieces and follow the same steps as for the pineapple in syrup.

Mini carrot cakes with cream cheese frosting

Preparation time: 20 minutes
Cooking time: 25 minutes
Makes 4–6 mini cakes

Base ingredients
100 g (3½ oz) plain flour, sifted
70 g (2½ oz) brown sugar
1 large carrot, finely grated
a handful of walnuts, roughly chopped
a handful of raisins
1 teaspoon cinnamon
1 egg
60 ml (2 fl oz) vegetable oil
2 scant teaspoons baking powder
a pinch of salt

Frosting ingredients
80 g (2¾ oz) butter
200 g (7 oz) cream cheese
100 g (3½ oz) icing sugar

Preheat the oven to 180°C (fan oven 160°C), Gas Mark 4.

Grease your cake moulds and dust with flour.

In a bowl, mix together the flour, sugar, carrot, walnuts, raisins, cinnamon and salt. In another bowl, beat the egg until it becomes frothy and firm. Add the oil little by little. You should get a mixture that starts to look a little like mayonnaise. Pour into the dry ingredients. Mix well. Add the baking powder.

As soon as you have stirred in the baking powder, divide the mixture between the moulds and put in the oven straight away.

Cook for around 30 minutes. Towards the end of the cooking time, keep an eye on the cakes and prick with a skewer if they seem ready. If it comes out clean, the cakes are done.

Leave in the tins to cool slightly before turning out.

While the cakes are cooking, prepare the frosting: beat the butter until smooth and quite soft. Do the same with the cream cheese. Once both ingredients are ready, mix together, adding the sugar bit by bit. If the mix is too grainy, put in the microwave for 2 seconds and mix again. Ice the cooled cakes with the frosting.

Mini spiced breads with chestnut flour

Preparation time: 20 minutes
Cooking time: 30 minutes
Makes 4–6 mini cakes

Base ingredients
500 ml (18 fl oz) milk
3 dessertspoons honey
2 eggs
20 g (¾ oz) icing sugar
100 g (3½ oz) chestnut flour
50 g (1¾ oz) plain flour, sifted
30 g (1 oz) butter, melted
2 teaspoons baking powder
a pinch of salt

Flavourings
50 g (1¾ oz) dried apricots,
   chopped
50 g (1¾ oz) figs, chopped
25 g (1 oz) hazelnuts, chopped
½ teaspoon allspice

Preheat the oven to 180°C (fan oven 160°C), Gas Mark 4.

Grease your cake moulds and dust with flour.

Gently heat the milk and honey and leave to melt.

In a large bowl, beat the eggs with the icing sugar until the mixture becomes pale and moussey.

Add the milk and honey little by little, then both flours and the butter.

Add the apricots, figs, hazelnuts, a pinch of salt and the allspice. Mix well.

Add the baking powder. As soon as you have done this, pour into the moulds and cook straight away for around 30 minutes.

Check the cakes are cooked by sticking a skewer in the middle, if it comes out clean, the cakes are done.

Leave in the tins to cool slightly before turning out.

Index

Conversion tables

The tables below are only approximate and are meant to be used as a guide only.

Approximate American/ European conversions

	USA	Metric	Imperial
brown sugar	1 cup	170 g	6 oz
butter	1 stick	115 g	4 oz
butter/ margarine/ lard	1 cup	225 g	8 oz
caster and granulated sugar	2 level tablespoons	30 g	1 oz
caster and granulated sugar	1 cup	225 g	8 oz
currants	1 cup	140 g	5 oz
flour	1 cup	140 g	5 oz
golden syrup	1 cup	350 g	12 oz
ground almonds	1 cup	115 g	4 oz
sultanas/ raisins	1 cup	200 g	7 oz

Approximate American/ European conversions

American	European
1 teaspoon	1 teaspoon/ 5 ml
½ fl oz	1 tablespoon/ ½ fl oz/ 15 ml
¼ cup	4 tablespoons/ 2 fl oz/ 50 ml
½ cup plus 2 tablespoons	¼ pint/ 5 fl oz/ 150 ml
1¼ cups	½ pint/ 10 fl oz/ 300 ml
1 pint/ 16 fl oz	1 pint/ 20 fl oz/ 600 ml
2½ pints (5 cups)	1.2 litres/ 2 pints
10 pints	4.5 litres/ 8 pints

Liquid measures

Imperial	ml	fl oz
1 teaspoon	5	
2 tablespoons	30	
4 tablespoons	60	
¼ pint/ 1 gill	150	5
⅓ pint	200	7
½ pint	300	10
¾ pint	425	15
1 pint	600	20
1¾ pints	1000 (1 litre)	35

Oven temperatures

American	Celsius	Fahrenheit	Gas Mark
Cool	130	250	½
Very slow	140	275	1
Slow	150	300	2
Moderate	160	320	3
Moderate	180	350	4
Moderately hot	190	375	5
Fairly hot	200	400	6
Hot	220	425	7
Very hot	230	450	8
Extremely hot	240	475	9

Other useful measurements

Measurement	Metric	Imperial
1 American cup	225 ml	8 fl oz
1 egg, size 3	50 ml	2 fl oz
1 egg white	30 ml	1 fl oz
1 rounded tablespoon flour	30 g	1 oz
1 rounded tablespoon cornflour	30 g	1 oz
1 rounded tablespoon caster sugar	30 g	1 oz
2 level teaspoons gelatine	10 g	¼ oz